Looking *for* Seabirds

Journal from an Alaskan Voyage

by Sophie Webb

 Houghton Mifflin

www.houghtonmifflinbooks.com

Book design by Lisa Diercks
The text of this book is set in Diotima and Marydale.
The illustrations are watercolor, gouache, and graphite.

Library of Congress Cataloging-in-Publication Data

Webb, Sophie.
    Looking for seabirds : journal from an Alaskan voyage / by Sophie Webb.
        p. cm.
Summary: A journal of the author's observations and adventures while working on a research vessel counting seabirds through Alaska's Aleutian Island chain.
    ISBN 0-618-21235-3 (hardcover)
    1. Sea birds—Alaska. 2. Webb, Sophie—Travel—Alaska. [1. Sea birds—Alaska. 2. Birds—Alaska. 3. Natural history—Alaska. 4. Diaries. 5. Alaska—Description and travel.] I. Title.
    QL684.A4W455 2004
    598.177'09798—dc22   2003012420

Printed in Singapore
TWP 10 9 8 7 6 5 4 3 2 1

For Larry Spear,

who has discovered so much about the lives of seabirds, and who has been both a teacher and an inspiration

Acknowledgments

There are so many people who helped with the making of this book that I begin with an apology to anyone I have forgotten. First, I thank George Hunt for the opportunity to work on one of his cruises in the Aleutians. Second, I thank Guy Guthridge from the National Science Foundation's Antarctic Artists and Writers Program: it was while on a cruise in the Antarctic on an NSF artists and writers grant that the idea of this book was conceived and several of the illustrations painted. I thank everyone I shared time with at sea during the past years, observing seabirds and marine mammals, in particular David Ainley, Lisa Ballance, Dawn Breese, Jim Cotton, Mike Force, Denise Hardesty, Steve Howell, Jaime Jahncke, Nina Karnovsky, Lori Mazzuca, Cornelia Oedekaven, Bob Pitman, Debi Shearwater, Larry Spear, and Suzanne Yin. I also must thank the captain and crew of the National Oceanic and Atmospheric Administration ship *David Starr Jordan*, who were all extremely helpful in answering my many questions about their various jobs, in particular Scott Hill, Jessica Kondel, Jose (Chico) Gomez, and Allen Gary. I also thank the captain and crew of the *Alpha Helix*, particularly Trish and all the scientists on the Aleutian trip. Josh Adams, Michelle Hester, Nina Karnovsky, Hannah Nevins, Lina Prairie, and Guy Tudor gave encouragement and helpful discussion. I'd like to thank PRBO for its continued support. Also the staff and founders of Oikonos: Grant Ballard, Tom Gardali, Sacha Heath, Michelle Hester, Carol Keiper, Hannah Nevins, and Viola Toniolo. Lastly, I thank Ann Rider, my editor, who read over numerous versions of the manuscript and made equally numerous helpful suggestions. Any mistakes in the information presented are entirely mine.

A Storm-Petrel, a seabird

Seabirds have always fascinated me. A diverse group, they spend the majority of their lives at sea, returning to land only to breed and perhaps occasionally to roost. One way I study seabirds is by observation; however, trying to study creatures that live on and in the deep ocean is difficult. How to see them?

Fortunately I have been able to work on several different research vessels as an observer, censusing, or counting, seabirds. I have been on cruises to the Arctic, the tip of South America, and the Antarctic. Some have been a couple weeks long, others a month or two. Now I am off to work for a month as a seabird observer for Dr. George Hunt along the Aleutian Island chain, in Alaska.

14 May 〜〜

I leave San Francisco at 9:30 A.M., flying to Seattle and then on to Anchorage, where I spend the night in a hotel. Anchorage is a flat city on the west coast of Alaska, with snow-capped mountains visible to the east.

15 May 〜〜

At 8:00 A.M. I am picked up by one of the oceanographers who will be on our cruise. He has with him two assistants. The car is stuffed with all the gear we'll need for the next month on the ship. The day is drizzly and gray, cold and unpleasant. It's hard to see much scenery on our way to Seward, where we'll meet the ship.

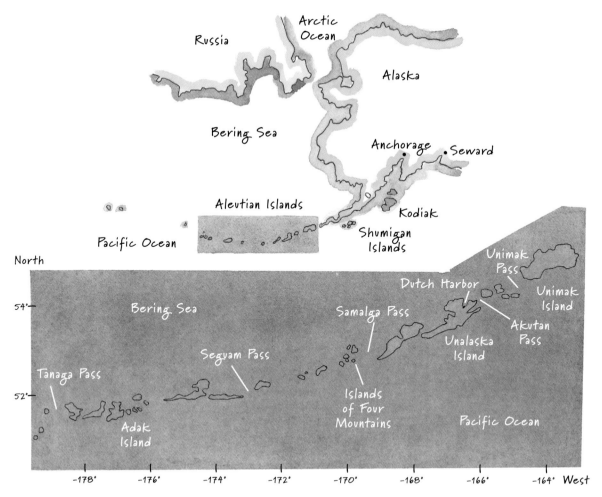

The area of our cruise through the Aleutian Islands in Alaska.

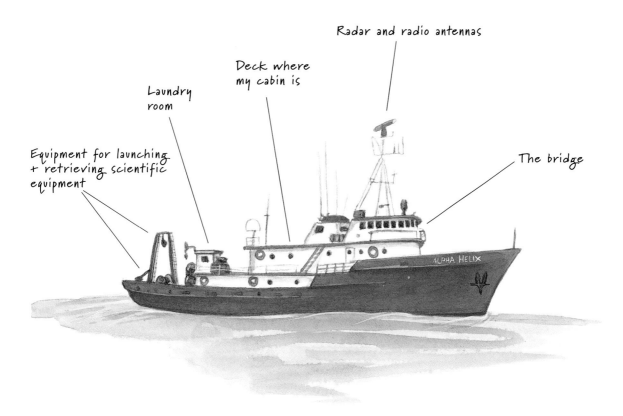

Radar and radio antennas

Deck where
my cabin is

Laundry
room

Equipment for launching
+ retrieving scientific
equipment

The bridge

ALPHA HELIX

The ALPHA HELIX: it's hard to believe it will be my home for a month.

We drive for three hours, arriving in Seward by 13:30 (or 1:30 P.M. — often when doing research, I use a twenty-four-hour clock). The *Alpha Helix*, our ship, is tied up at the University of Alaska dock at the far end of town. Only 133 feet long, it just doesn't look big enough for the twenty-two people who will be on it, as well as all the various projects and equipment. We unload the car and carry our luggage onto the ship. The cabin I'm in is quite nice, although I do need to share it with three other scientists. At least it's above deck and has two portholes, so there is light. On some ships I've ended up in a cabin below decks, with no natural light. Entering that sort of cabin always feels like entering a cave.

Once we're unpacked it's time to see the town. Seward has one main street with several bars, restaurants, and tourist gift shops. We wander about and have our last dinner on land for a month. Then it's back to the ship for bed. The weather begins to clear in the afternoon. Seward is quite beautiful, situated at the end of Resurrection Bay. Snow-capped forested mountains flank each side of the bay.

16 May

The day dawns absolutely beautiful: sunny, clear, and calm. After a delay the engines start their rumbling to warm up, then their roar, and we leave Seward by 10:00 A.M. We travel ten to fifteen miles off the coast.

The main purpose of this cruise is to investigate possible causes of the population decline of the Steller's sea lion. We are trying to discover whether this decline is due to killer whale predation or lack of available food. We also want to know where in the Aleutians there is an abundance of food and what causes the abundance. The project then has several components that will help us understand the Aleutian Island system better: oceanography, marine biology, mammalogy, and ornithology. My job falls under ornithology: I census seabirds. Seabirds can be indicators of the availability of food to animals that feed high in the food chain, like Steller's sea lions.

So what are seabirds, exactly? They are birds that live on the ocean. Some of these birds are familiar to us, such as penguins, albatross, and puffins. But there are also the less familiar: boobies and gannets, shearwaters, storm-petrels (one of my favorites), petrels, auklets, and murres. There are even two species of shorebirds, phalaropes, that spend much of their life on the ocean.

Some seabirds: a Red-footed Booby from the tropics, a Parakeet Auklet from the Arctic, and a Rockhopper Penguin from the Antarctic.

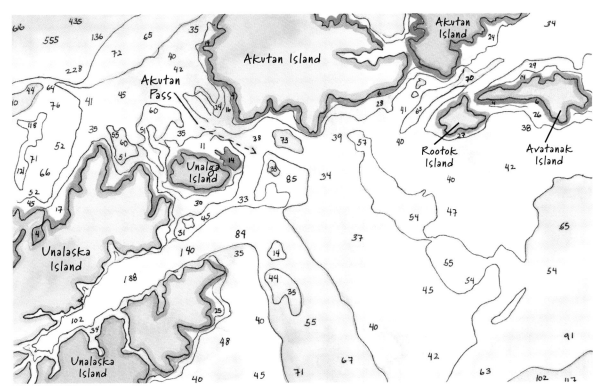

This chart shows the bathymetry, or geography and contours, of the sea floor around several of the Aleutian Islands.

Seabirds, like whales and dolphins and all other truly marine species, are difficult to study at sea. Our knowledge of them in their pelagic (open ocean) environment is increasing, but it is still small in comparison with our knowledge of them at their breeding colonies. And there are even several species of seabirds whose breeding grounds remain a mystery.

It feels great to be out on the ocean again, looking at birds. To really understand seabirds it is important to consider how the ocean might look to them. The ocean from our viewpoint looks fairly uniform, but to the birds it is a mosaic of habitats, just as the land is to us. Important considerations for birds are distance from land, underwater geography (or bathymetry), water temperature and depth, currents, and shelf breaks (an area at the edge of the continental shelf where there is often a great deal of upwelling, a mixing warm and cooler, nutrient-filled water). All these factors can affect where one finds seabirds. When traveling on a ship we make transects through these different habitats and can therefore encounter a variety of birds.

So why is it important to understand bird distribution in the ocean? Seabirds could help warn us about a change in the health of the ocean. Imagine if a bird population dropped drastically in a certain area; it could indicate that there is a severe decline in the productivity, or food supply, in the ocean for some reason. An El Niño event (a natural warming of the Pacific Ocean that can be mild or drastic depending on the year) might have occurred, or an oil spill, or some other less detectable pollutant might have been introduced into the ocean. Seabirds are very sensitive to these changes, particularly during the breeding season, when they require greater amounts of food to feed their growing chicks.

Today there are a few birds about in small groups. The majority are in the family (a grouping of birds that share common characteristics) Alcidae. Alcids include the puffins, murres, murrelets, and auklets. They are one of the main reasons I wanted to go on this research cruise to the Aleutians. Alcids live only in the northern hemisphere and are thought to be the ecological counterpart of the penguins, found in the southern hemisphere. Much like penguins, they are predominantly black and white, and it is

Adélie Penguins of the Antarctic look superficially similar to the Thick-billed and Common Murres of the Arctic.

really their face, size, and bill color that separate them from each other. Like the penguins, they generally prefer cool water and spend most of the year at sea, going to remote islands or coastal areas only to breed. They feed on crustaceans (small relatives of the shrimp) and fish. Unlike penguins, however, they can fly. When they have their breeding plumage, the alcids have a variety of facial tufts and plumes, which give them a rather bizarre appearance. They are fun to look at and draw.

Here are seven alcids often seen in the Aleutians.

Alcids are also found along the Pacific coast of the United States. Although primarily ocean species, many kinds of alcids feed in what is called the neritic zone. This is the area from the coast out to the edge of the continental shelf. Because it is close to land, this zone is susceptible to a number of negative encounters with humans. There is evidence, for example, that the Common Murre population in California has declined because of oil spills, drownings in nets (birds get caught in the nets when diving for fish and drown), and a reduction in the fish they feed their chicks. Perhaps the most difficult challenge in all the world's oceans is their gradual degradation by human pollution, plastic litter, and overfishing.

Today there are lots of snazzy-looking Tufted Puffins floating on the water in pairs. It is the beginning of their breeding season. There is also a scattering of small flocks of Red Phalaropes in breeding plumage. These odd shorebirds have lobed

Tufted Puffins: they are one of the more common species on this trip. They also breed as far south as the Farallon Islands off San Francisco. They are the clowns of the sea.

Three Red Phalaropes sit on the water: two females and a male. Phalaropes are one of the exceptions in the bird world: the female is more brightly colored than the male. She lays the eggs in the nest and then leaves. The male incubates the eggs and raises the chicks.

toes for swimming. They breed in the high Arctic tundra (flat, sparsely vegetated, treeless terrain that has permanently frozen soil) and winter on the ocean as far south as Chile.

Many species migrate to the Arctic to breed and feed, for in the summer there is an incredible increase of food in the Arctic Ocean. This bloom is caused by the periodic mixing of water due to storms, upwelling, and freshwater flow from the annual melting of snow and ice as the region warms. Nutrients from the land and sea floor are mixed into the water. The addition of these nutrients, combined with a long period of daylight, promotes the growth of tiny plants called phytoplankton, which feed small animals called zooplankton. The zooplankton are then eaten by fish, birds, marine mammals, and on up the food chain.

This pair of Crested Auklets, with their big orange smiling beaks and forward-pointing plumes, looks like something out of Dr. Seuss's imagination. A volcano looms up out of the water, the snow dripping down like melting buttercream frosting. A white plume of steam billows from the peak of this still active volcano. Streams of Crested Auklets fly by, their beaks almost fluorescent in the light. A sperm whale spouts in the distance.

At sea my favorite time of day is sunrise. It can be beautiful, and there is always the anticipation of the unexpected: What will we see today?

18 May

On this cruise we will travel about three quarters of the way out the Aleutian Island chain. The name comes from the Native American people who used to inhabit the islands: the Aleuts. The chain extends for about 1,200 miles, and separates the Pacific Ocean from the Bering Sea. Many of the Aleutian Islands are rocky and mountain-ous, and several have active volcanoes.

It is a cold morning, though quite calm, as we pass by the Shumigan Islands. Not quite to the Aleutians yet.

One thing I like about ship life is that my days are always busy and planned. I get up before dawn, have breakfast, and then go up to the bridge or flying bridge when the sun begins to rise. From there I do my seabird observations until dusk.

Most of the research vessels I have been on are fairly large, ranging from 170 to

220 feet in length. The day-to-day running of such a large marine research vessel is complex. The ship and equipment must be maintained in good working order to ensure both safety and the completion of the scientific projects. Cruise schedules must be planned and meals must be served on time (and be tasty), even in rough weather. Quite a crew of people is needed to run a research ship, from the captain, to the bosun (in charge of deck hands), engineers, and cooks. And then there are the scientific personnel. The ship can be a crowded place.

Living on a ship is like living in a very small town — except that the floor is always moving, particularly if there's wind and the ship becomes bouncy, and the engines are always running. After the first couple days I get used to their constant droning, but every once in a while, particularly when trying to sleep, I become conscious of how noisy they are. Once we have docked somewhere and the engines are shut off, I feel relieved: it's so quiet!

The captain and one of his mates on the bridge. The captain plans out the ship's course daily. He is also responsible for ensuring the safety of all personnel and the ship, managing the ship's budget, planning out the sailing schedule with the scientists, training the junior officers and personnel, and overseeing the crew.

As we head out from the lee (protection) of the islands, the winds increase from 15 knots to 35. The seas become progressively bumpier, with whitecaps littering the gray ocean. Mountains on the islands have clouds over them and a dark gray forbidding sky. Once we are completely outside of the islands, things begin to rock and roll. We turn so we are lying in the trough. With its rounded bottom the *Helix* rolls from side to side. Immediately

My bunk is a refuge, one of the few places I can be away from other people (if I pull the curtains closed!).

we know what hasn't been tied down as things go skittering off tables and objects in drawers and closets go *bang* to one side, and then *bang* to the other. As the ship sways it's hard to walk and, at times, even to just sit and read. I spend part of the day on the bridge looking for birds, but soon the roll and the rain and fog make observations impossible. I go to the small ship's library where there are a few desks and try to draw and paint for fun, but that too is impossible. So I head back to my cabin and lie down to read. The ship is pitching so much that even in my bunk it's hard to remain stationary. Fortunately, I don't feel ill, just sleepy and worn out by the weather. I often have to contend with feeling mildly seasick for the first few days at sea. But fairly quickly I gain my "sea legs." On these bouncy days even small tasks become difficult. I usually end up with black and blue bruises from knocking against a wall or a ladder (the name for stairs on the ship) between decks. Even taking a shower can be an event as the ship rocks back and forth. The soap goes shooting out of my hand, lands on the floor, and then becomes almost impossible to pick up without falling down, which results in more bruises and soap in my eyes. But it's always worth a little discomfort to be out on the ocean.

We have an uncomfortable, pitching night. It is hard to sleep as we're tossed about in our bunks.

19 May ～◯

By 1:00 to 2:00 A.M. the seas calm down and sleep is possible. For those who were seasick yesterday, it's a welcome relief.

The day is cold and gray as we head into Dutch Harbor on Unalaska Island. It's a small and desolate fishing town. Tied up to the dock are many trawlers from ports in Alaska and the northwest coast of the United States. We arrive at about 7:30 A.M. We will be here only long enough to offload some equipment for a future cruise and pick up the rest of the scientific party: marine mammal, seabird, and marine biologists and oceanographers. By 10:00 A.M. we are listening to our second pre-cruise safety lecture and trying on our survival suits. And then we're steaming out. The weather is overcast and dead calm. Winds are 5 knots from the north. Now there are at least three observers on the bridge at all times — one bird observer and two marine mammal observers.

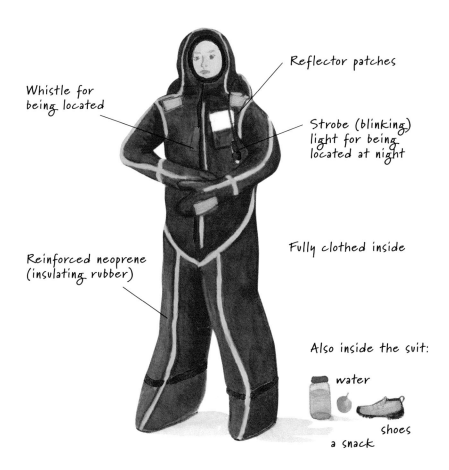

Reflector patches

Whistle for being located

Strobe (blinking) light for being located at night

Reinforced neoprene (insulating rubber)

Fully clothed inside

Neoprene survival suits are tried on once a month. They are awkward and bulky, but they might save our lives if we have to abandon ship in the frigid Arctic water. We wear them only if we abandon ship.

Also inside the suit:

water

a snack

shoes

17

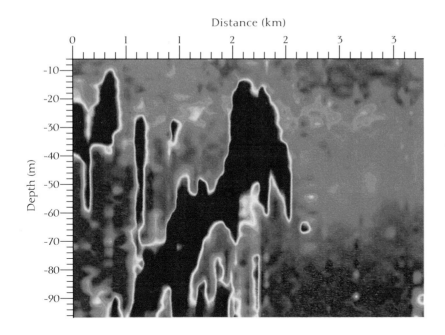

Distance (km)

Depth (m)

A graph from the acoustic array. The red areas indicate the presence of zoo- plankton: copepods and krill. They are small crustaceans that fish, birds, and whales feed on.

20 May

Today we are making a transit through Unimak Pass, one area of our study. In the passes there are often concentrations of birds. We want our transit through the pass to coincide with the tide so that we will cross where there is a mixing of colder Bering Sea water and warmer water from the Pacific. This is called a tidal front. Here, the mixing of water stirs up nutrients from the sea floor, creating food for a bloom of phytoplank- ton, which in turn are eaten by zooplankton. Also at the front there can be huge groupings of zooplankton that get pushed together into a con- centrated area. In the food-rich water of these convergence zones there are often hundreds to thousands of birds feeding on the zooplankton and fish.

copepod

We are towing an acoustic array. It is a digi- tal echo sounder that sends out beams of sound at different frequencies. Since different- size objects create different patterns and are picked up by different frequencies, we will get an idea of what's in the water. We can tell, for example, the density of krill or copepods. The cable from the acoustic array conducts this information to a computer on the ship.

krill

While the acoustic array is being towed we census birds. We count them in what is called a strip transect. One can't look everywhere at the same time, so we restrict ourselves to a quadrant from the middle of the ship to 90 degrees of the beam and out to 300 meters. Beyond 300 meters, high winds or glare off the water make it difficult to identify the smaller birds.

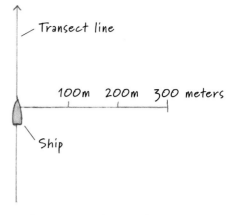

Our census transect

Despite the drizzle we do see some interesting birds. A surprise long-distance migrant appears out of nowhere: a Mottled Petrel, a bird that breeds on islands near New Zealand in the southern hemisphere. The bird floats in the air. Petrels are some of the most graceful fliers in the world.

A Mottled Petrel flies by the ship. In the distance are snow-covered volcanic peaks, one a perfect cone. A hint of a rosy dawn sky fingers its way through the clouds.

The tubenoses: note how the tubes lie on top of the bill of most species but are inset into the bill of the albatross.

Short-tailed Albatross

Mottled Petrel

Northern Fulmar

Leach's Storm-Petrel

Short-tailed Shearwater

Petrels are in a group of birds commonly called the tubenoses. Other kinds in this group are the albatross, storm-petrels, and shearwaters. They are called tubenoses because their nostrils are either encased in tubes that lie on top of their bill or embedded in their bill. The birds excrete salty water through these tubes. Because they eat only food from the salty ocean, they continuously swallow salt with the food they eat, and so must rid themselves of the salt. Also, like all animals they need fresh water. So in their foreheads they have salt glands that help remove salt from the ocean water. The salty water runs out the tubes, giving the birds a constant "nasal drip" at the end of their beak.

One of the great albatross of the southern oceans, the Royal Albatross, has a tremendous wingspan of more than 11 feet. Royal Albatross mate for life and live fifty years or more.

22 May 〜⊙

Yesterday we spent heading west to Akutan Pass. This morning the seas are glassy, but by the afternoon the wind picks up. There aren't very many birds around, though in one area there are at least twenty-five Laysan Albatross, ten Black-footed Albatross, and one immature Short-tailed Albatross, quite blotchy with a yellow head.

Albatross are tubenoses like the petrels and are the giants of the bird world. Albatross fly by dynamic soaring: riding the eddies and currents made by the wind as it travels over the water. Studies have shown that during this type of flight albatross use about the same amount of energy as they would sitting on the water! They are some of the most impressive birds to watch fly. They are simply huge.

Most albatross are found in the southern hemisphere. A band of constant wind travels around the bottom of the globe with virtually no obstruction, so the albatross can just set their wings and fly. But three species of Albatross breed and are found regularly in the northern hemisphere: the Black-footed, Laysan and Short-tailed Albatross, just what we've seen today. The Black-footed and Laysan both breed in the tropical climate of the Hawaiian Island chain and Mexico. The Short-tailed, the rarest of the three species, breeds only on Tori Shima Island off of Japan. Its population was severely reduced, to possibly only ten pairs, by the feather trade of the nineteenth century. Only recently has its population begun to increase to about 1,200 individuals. I was very excited to see the immature Short-tailed Albatross today.

The three northern hemisphere albatross: Short-tailed, Black-footed, and two Laysans.

All albatross take years to mature, starting to breed at six to ten years old. For most of those years they remain at sea, perhaps visiting a colony one to two years before first breeding. They feed predominantly on fish, squid, and carrion (rotting meat, such as a dead whale). The latter they find by their acute sense of smell, another characteristic of the tubenoses. Unfortunately the long-line fishery has severely affected albatross populations. Long-line boats fish for a variety of fish, ranging from cod and tuna to halibut. They put out lines of baited hooks, a mile to several miles long. When albatross try to eat either the bait or the fish, they can get caught on the hooks. As the line is being hauled in or let out, they drown.

The Light-mantled Sooty Albatross is one of the most graceful and beautiful of all seabirds. It breeds on sub-Antarctic Islands.

A Laysan Albatross on its nest on Laysan Island in the warm tropical Hawaiian Island chain—quite a contrast to their feeding area in misty, cold Alaska.

By attaching satellite radio transmitters to Laysan and Black-footed Albatross, scientists have found that albatross fly to Alaskan waters all the way from the Hawaiian Islands to find food to bring back to their chicks! The satellite transmitter sends a GPS (global positioning system) point to the satellite, which then sends information to a computer that will log the coordinates of the bird's location. The trip to Alaska from Hawaii and back may take ten days to two weeks, covering a distance of 9,000 kilometers (about 5,600 miles).

Because albatross fly such long distances, they cannot carry too much weight. But they need to bring back large quantities of food to their chicks. So the birds convert the fish and squid they catch into a thick, smelly oil. The mass and weight of the oil is much less than those of fish or squid. When the albatross return to their chicks, they regurgitate the oil into their awaiting beaks. They also puke the oil on intruders as a defense mechanism. It is disgusting to be puked on when handling a bird.

25 May

Gray and rainy with fairly big swells today. The winds increase from 15 to 25 knots in the afternoon. We spend the day doing a CTD line. This is an instrument used to gather water. Ten to twenty cylindrical bottles are lowered to the desired depth, which can be 500 meters or more, and then are slowly raised to varying depths. The bottles gather water samples and are electronically closed at each depth. Oceanographers then analyze the water in each bottle for chlorophyll, nutrients (nitrate, nitrite, silicate, and phosphate), and salts. This information tells us about the physics and biology of the area where the water was collected.

There are CTD stations every forty minutes. Northern Fulmars (also tubenoses) are starting to follow and surround the ship.

The ship is pitching and rolling. It's about 11:00 P.M., and we're stopped at a station to do a CTD. The dull roar of the engines is a constant background noise. Soon I'll hear the increase of rpm's, a vibration and a louder roar as the ship begins to gather speed and move on to the next CTD station. The ride will get even rougher. Hope we can sleep! The oceanographers often work through the night.

The CTD being lowered on a windy day. CTD stands for conductivity, temperature, and depth.

Northern Fulmars are scavengers. They look for anything edible that might be thrown from the galley (kitchen) and, I hate to say, flushed from the bilges (that is, human waste — yuck).

27 May

Spent the day traveling west along the south side of the Aleutian chain. Although skies are thick with clouds and there is spitting rain, the seas are calm to glassy, like liquid mercury, reflecting the birds flying above. As we head west the mornings begin later but the nights become shorter, so our daylight is now from about 7:00 A.M. to midnight. Long work days: we sometimes observe until just before dark.

We cross several tidal fronts and eddies on our transit. At one front there are thousands of foraging Northern Fulmars. They sit on the water in dense flocks, feeding on copepods at the surface.

There is one flock of 150 Ancient Murrelets. Like the puffins and auklets, these small birds are alcids. Ancient Murrelets breed in the Aleutians. When their chicks are only a few days old the adults lead them from their burrow or crevasse nest to the ocean. These tiny balls of down have to walk across roots and boulders to the sea and then negotiate the surf to follow their calling parents. They will remain at sea with them for several weeks as they molt their down, grow their first coat of feathers, and learn how to feed.

We are now near Seguam Pass.

Ancient Murrelets are common breeders in the Aleutian Islands. Their chicks go to sea as tiny balls of fluff.

On most ships I do my observations from the flying bridge, outside on the top of the ship. There I have to contend with wind, rain, and sea spray. Usually there is a chair and a mounted plastic box to protect my portable computer (for data entry).

29 May

Overcast and gray with a lumpy sea and swells. The winds are 15 knots all day. Good thing we do our observation from the bridge, rather than the flying bridge. If we were outside, the drizzle and rain would make us cold and miserable.

We go over an underwater pinnacle (a large rock outcrop rising from the sea floor) and encounter a tidal front. The tides here are very strong, moving at speeds of 5 knots or more, and help mix the warmer Pacific water with the colder Bering Sea water. The Least Auklets nest in the hundreds of thousands on some of the islands in the Aleutians. The only way they can be sure to have enough food to take back and feed all those chicks is to nest in areas associated with the tidal fronts. The fronts, as long as the system remains relatively undisturbed, guarantee available food.

There are Least Auklets
everywhere feeding along
the tidal front today.

The Least Auklets, like the fulmars, are feeding almost exclusively on copepods. There are thousands of Least Auklets littering the ocean here, like insects. They whirr about in flocks as the ship flushes them off the water. It is an incredible sight. The ocean is teeming with little round feathered and winged balls zooming about everywhere. They are adorable.

It is exhausting censusing all the auklets, and confusing. With these large numbers of birds, censusing becomes a team effort: Jaime, a graduate student from Peru, records, I count the Least Auklets, and George, my boss, counts anything different. I get so excited and stressed that my binoculars steam up. I call out "525, 150, 250, 75, 85" to Jaime, as he busily types the information into the portable computer.

The activity stops almost as abruptly as it started. The area of high productivity is narrow, and we have traveled through it. Just a memory now, it is one of those wonderful events in the natural world, completely overwhelming. This is what I came north to see.

30 May ∿⟩

Another gray day with rain. Seas go from calm to rolling to calm to rolling. We spend the day in Tanaga Pass, the farthest west we will go. The water is quite deep in spots and again there is a distinct tidal front. There are not as many Least Auklets as yesterday, but as we did yesterday we are seeing Fork-tailed Storm-Petrels feeding on one side of the tidal front, Least Auklets on the other.

Two species of storm-petrels commonly found along the Aleutian chain are Fork-tailed and Leach's. Storm-petrels are one of my favorite groups. They are found in most regions of the world's oceans, particularly where the water is cooler. Most are small sparrow-size birds, usually brown and often with a broad white band across their rump. My first encounter with storm-petrels was many years ago when I was working on a National Oceanic and Atmospheric Administration (NOAA) ship off the coast of Massachusetts. That trip began my lifelong fascination with these tiny birds that spend their life far out in the ocean, returning to land only to breed.

The birds I saw off the coast of Massachusetts were Wilson's Storm-Petrels, birds I would encounter again in the Pacific Ocean off California and soaring above my head in the far south of the Antarctic. Wilson's Storm-Petrels are widespread, perhaps one of the most numerous seabirds in the world.

On a cruise to the Antarctic I saw and painted this Wilson's Storm-Petrel pattering on the sea's surface near an ice floe.

Fork-tailed and Leach's Storm-Petrels: both of these species breed in Alaska.

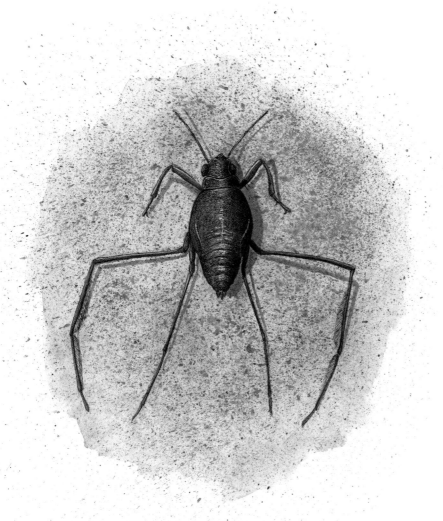

HALOBATES is the only pelagic (ocean water) insect. It is related to the water striders one often sees skittering across pond surfaces or large puddles. HALOBATES "stride" over the surface of the ocean. They are often eaten by storm-petrels in the tropics.

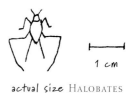

actual size HALOBATES

Several species of storm-petrels are commonly seen thousands of miles from shore, feeding on creatures found on the ocean's surface: *Halobates* (the only true marine insect), small Portuguese men-of-war (jellyfish that are highly toxic to us), copepods, krill, and a variety of other zooplankton. Storm-petrels' extraordinary sense of smell helps them search for food. Sometimes they will find a rotting whale carcass floating and will gather about it in the thousands, feeding on the oozing oils and bits of flesh.

How do these tiny birds, out thousands of miles, manage to survive severe storms, buffeted by the wind? Sometimes there are huge landings of them along the coast, called wrecks, during hurricanes. I imagine, though, that they usually survive by fluttering in the wind or bobbing on the waves.

Leach's Storm-Petrels breed in the Arctic but also on islands off California and Baja California in Mexico. They nest in burrows. One night on an island in Baja I heard a pair dueting from inside their burrow: long rolling, rising, and falling trills. This is what I imagined they looked like snuggled together, singing, in their burrow.

At night, bright lights from the ship attract and confuse storm-petrels, like moths attracted to a flame. If they land on the ship, they are unable to fly off, needing a ledge, small cliff, or unobstructed flat water to take off from. Their legs, designed for paddling on the ocean, are set far back on their bodies and are neither strong nor made for walking. The scientists working at night catch them and put them in a box so I can look at and release them in the morning. If they are left on the deck they can get hurt. Often they disappear under some equipment, looking for the safety of a burrow (similar to the way they nest), and become trapped or get oil on their feathers, which makes them unable to fly or stay warm (feathers are good insulation and oil destroys them). Then they can die.

A Leach's Storm-Petrel attracted to a light on the ship.

A large, three-inch plastic lure for catching fish or squid lodged in the rib cage of a Laysan Albatross. It probably caused the albatross to die. I saw this on Laysan Island when I was working on a cruise in the Hawaiian Island chain.

Seabirds have been on the earth much longer than we have. But with the advent of humans and the huge increase in our population, seabirds face new challenges. On land, the introduction of goats, rabbits, cats, and rats to remote islands has severely affected the birds' breeding populations. On the ocean, plastic has become a hazard for all marine creatures. To seabirds, floating bits of plastic and Styrofoam beads can look like small jellyfish or zooplankton. Plastic lures and floats can look like squid or fish. The seabirds are fooled and they eat them. Because plastic doesn't break down, it will eventually cause blockages in the digestive tract. I am always surprised that even a thousand miles from land I see floating Styrofoam cups, plastic buoys, and drifting pieces of nylon fishing net on the ocean.

06 June ~⁀

Overcast and windy, perhaps 35 knots. Fairly big waves, about 13 feet, and the swell causes the ship to rock and sway.

The CTD line gathering oceanographic information is finished by midmorning. Now we are racing for shelter to the lee of an island. The winds are supposed to pick up.

Last night in the cabin while we were getting ready for bed, the swells increased. There is always something loose that, once everyone is in bed and the ship starts swaying, begins its periodic knocking, just loud enough to be irritating but not so annoying that one has to get out of the bunk immediately. Then finally the search begins: Is it the cup? The handle of some mounted binoculars knocking against the wall? The porthole cover bouncing up and down? A can in the trash? Some shoes in the closet? Ah, it's the binoculars this time.

A shower, today, is out of the question, but it is time for lunch. I go down the ladder near my cabin to the mess.

On the ship the chief steward has a difficult job. He or she has to plan three meals a day for twenty-five to thirty-five people for at least a month and then order all the supplies and make sure they are stored properly so that they won't spoil before the end of the trip. They also have to accommodate different eating needs and habits, from vegetarians to people from different cultures. (On many cruises researchers from several different countries collaborate on projects). There is a set meal schedule and always lots of, often too many, snacks and freshly baked cakes, pies, and cookies about — constant temptation.

A male Lapland Longspur lands on the ship to rest. Lapland Longspurs are migrant land birds, similar to sparrows, that winter across the lower forty-eight states. In the spring they fly north to breed in the Arctic tundra. They have a lovely song.

The mess. This is where we eat all our meals and often gather to play Scrabble or cards, watch videos, and chat in the evenings and during breaks.

Somehow rougher seas often seem to coincide with meals of round food. So I find myself chasing peas, carrots, or new potatoes about my plate as we roll from side to side. Mashed potatoes would be a wiser choice. But today the steward has made a sensible pan of enchiladas that remain flat on my plate. A big swell hits and the galley porthole darkens as the rail of the ship dips into the sea. Lunch begins to fly out of the hot trays where it is nestled. It's hard to do much on a day like today. A sort of sleepy fog descends on me — my version of getting seasick.

Some of the birds, the fulmars and albatross, thrive in the wind: soaring and whipping across the ocean and by the ship. They are amazing. The winds are nothing to them, yet so uncomfortable to us.

We steam behind the Islands of Four Mountains to rest and hide from the wind.

It is quiet and protected here. The islands are noticeably greener than when we passed by earlier. Summer has arrived.

09 June ∽

Samalga Pass. The day started off overcast and windy and became partly clear and calm. The birds here are all tubenoses: Northern Fulmars, Laysan Albatross, and Black-footed Albatross, with a few scattered flocks of Short-tailed Shearwaters. There is an increase in the number of Black-footed Albatross from when we were in this area three weeks ago. We pass by an island with a colony (breeding group) of about a hundred Stellar's Sea Lions. They look like enormous pale sausages lying about on the rocks. We haven't seen many sea lions feeding in the passes, only a few small colonies on scattered islands. Tomorrow we return to Unimak Pass.

16 June ∽

We have only a couple days left on the cruise. After thirty days at sea I think everyone is ready to get off the ship. Some strong personalities and tempers have begun to show in the close living situation of ship life. Most of us are stir-crazy, and the weather has been miserable for most of the trip.

After an acoustic array survey through Akutan Pass, we head east along the north shore of Akutan Island toward Unimak Pass. We find a huge area of productivity: swarms of krill balling at the surface, pink patches in the water. Looking down into the water column, we see layers and layers of krill. There are thousands of schooling fish, herring perhaps, and below them silver flashes of larger fish, possibly salmon. An even more impressive sight, though, are the hundred Humpback Whales and the one to two million Short-tailed Shearwaters feeding here. It is impossible to estimate the number of birds. A massive cloud of birds, layer upon layer, swirls up and obscures a distant ship. Flocks on the water leapfrog and dive in a dense, intense mass. In the sky they look like swarming gnats. As the ship moves through the flocks on the water I can hear the pattering of their feet and wings as they try to take off out of the ship's way. Their nasal calls are barely audible over the sound of the ship's engines. To lighten their load in order to fly, they vomit their recently acquired meal of krill. Humpback Whales lunge feed, coming out of the water head first, their mouths wide open, throats extended, and water streaming out through their baleen. It is an incredible sight.

Short-tailed Shearwaters are long-distance migrants. They breed on islands off Australia during the austral summer (the Arctic/northern winter). Humpback Whales are migrants too. They breed in the warm waters off Hawaii and Mexico. Both species migrate to Alaska to feed on the abundance of food that occurs in the Arctic summer.

Seabirds sometimes rest on floating objects. Above are Common Murres on kelp, and below a Nazca Booby on the back of a green sea turtle in the tropics.

18 June ∿〜

Unimak Pass. Our second to last night at sea. The weather is good, overcast but with flat seas. We travel up from the south along the southwest side of Unalaska Island.

We pass several groups of murres standing about on kelp (seaweed). Out on the ocean I frequently see birds resting on floating objects: terns on drifting buoys or a booby on the back of a sea turtle.

The day ends with a transit through Unimak Pass for another census of birds. There are not many birds besides the familiar Northern Fulmars, Thick-billed and Common Murres, Ancient Murrelets, and Short-tailed Shearwaters. I will miss these birds. But a few fulmars and murres may spend part of the winter in the ocean off central California, where I live. So I hope to see some of them again soon.

44

We offload our gear and say goodbye to the ALPHA HELIX.

20 June 〜

We have arrived in Dutch Harbor. By 8:00 A.M. we're off the ship and preparing to go home. The stable earth feels odd beneath my feet. Some people experience "dock rock" and are ill for the first few hours back on land. But it feels good to be able to walk, and although Dutch Harbor is bleak there seems to be so much to look at after a month of gray ocean and sparse islands.

In a couple of months most of the seabirds will leave Alaskan waters. The albatross, petrels, and shearwaters will fly south to breed. The albatross will fly to islands off Japan, Hawaii, and Mexico, the petrels and shearwaters to islands off Australia and New Zealand. Many of the alcids, the fulmars, storm-petrels, and phalaropes, will also go south for the winter: the fulmars and storm-petrels to the Pacific Ocean off the western United States and the tiny phalaropes as far south as the ocean off Chile. Next spring they will all return again to Alaskan waters for the incredible bloom of food.

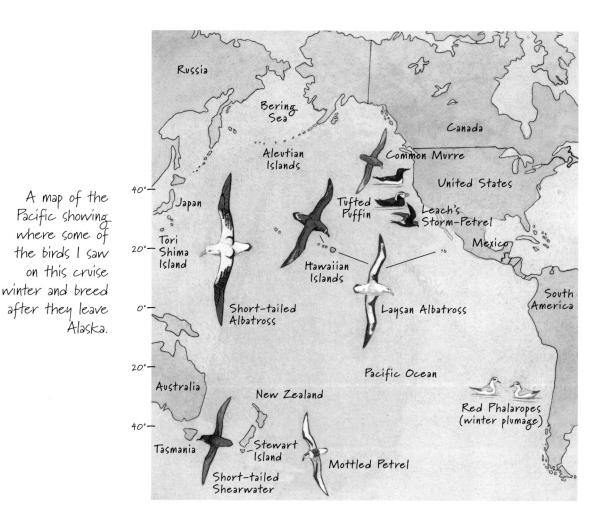

A map of the Pacific showing where some of the birds I saw on this cruise winter and breed after they leave Alaska.

On this trip not only have I seen huge numbers of birds and even a few rare birds but I've also learned more about the dynamics of the Arctic marine ecosystem. The information that we have gathered will be analyzed and added to a database from previous years. Providing more information will help us make wise marine management decisions in the region and will add to the scientific knowledge of the ecosystem.

Every time I go out on the ocean I am reminded of how complex it is, how it is a patchwork of different environments. Also, as time goes on I am made increasingly aware of how fragile the ocean is. It is not limitless, and we humans must be good stewards and ensure that the ecosystems remain healthy. I look forward to my next journey out to sea, this time to the warm waters of the eastern tropical Pacific, to continue learning more about the ocean and the wonderful seabirds that live on it.

Some of the birds seen during the cruise

47